ROSAMOND RICHARDSON

Vegetarian

ROSAMOND RICHARDSON

Vegetarian

Photography by Philip Wilkins

WEIDENFELD & NICOLSON

Rosamond Richardson

Rosamond Richardson has written numerous cookery books. *Alfresco*, her book on eating out of doors, won the entertaining category of the James Beard Awards in 1993. *The Great Green Cookbook* has received widespread acclaim, and *Food from Green Places* was published in 1997. Rosamond was also food consultant for Linda McCartney's best-selling *Linda's Kitchen*. She lives in a small village in the Essex countryside.

Contents

WATERCRESS SOUP 10

MUSHROOM AND PESTO TARTLETS 12

MIXED SALAD LEAVES WITH SESAME DRESSING AND SHAVED PARMESAN 14

TINY SPINACH SOUFFLÉS 16

POLENTA WITH SUN-DRIED TOMATOES AND MOZZARELLA 18

CHINESE NOODLES WITH BROCCOLI, GINGER AND BLACK BEAN SAUCE 20

COUSCOUS WITH SPICY LEEKS AND TOMATOES 22

PENNE WITH RED AND YELLOW PEPPER SAUCE 24

CHIMICHANGAS WITH SALSA 26

BUTTERNUT SQUASH GRATIN 28

STIR-FRIED MANGETOUT AND MUSHROOMS 30

WHITE CHOCOLATE ANGEL GATEAU 32

THE BASICS

Béchamel sauce 34

Pesto 34

Vegetable stock 35

Polenta 36

Couscous 36

Cooking pasta 37

Ginger 37

He may live without books –
what is knowledge but grieving?

He may live without hope –
what is hope but deceiving?

He may live without love –
what is passion but pining?

But civilised man cannot live
without dining.

OWEN, EARL OF LYTTON,
1831–1891

Introduction

As we approach the end of the second millennium a new world of vegetarian cookery has opened up, shedding its old skin of brown rice and sandals. Cuisines of every culture, which have always had their repertoire of meatless dishes, have contributed to the current of modern cookery as world communications systems have dissolved distances. The speed of international haulage has meant that day-fresh fruits and vegetables can be transported to supermarkets all over the globe, vastly increasing our choices, as well as defying the seasons. Alongside this trend the organic movement has been gaining momentum and finding more and more outlets for its untouched-by-chemicals products. There is also an increasing interest in the 'potager' or kitchen garden, in growing your own on little plots of land, and a surprising return to country markets where you can buy freshly picked seasonal produce. The food that you can cook from the wonderful and colourful variety of vegetables through the seasons and around the world is as beautiful to look at as it is delicious – and healthy – to eat.

To select just a dozen recipes from so many traditions has been a great joy: I have winged my way – and with apologies for all the sins of omission – to American, French, Italian, Chinese, North African and Mexican cuisines, as I made this brief culinary journey around the globe.

Rosmund Richardson

WATERCRESS SOUP

**SERVES 2 AS A MEAL,
4 AS A STARTER**

675 g/1½ lb potatoes,
  cut into chunks
900 ml/1½ pints vegetable
  stock (page 35), or water
  and 2 vegetable stock cubes
100 g/3½ oz watercress,
  washed
freshly grated nutmeg
salt and pepper
150 ml/5 fl oz single cream
  or milk

Put the potatoes in a saucepan with the stock or water and bring to the boil. Pull off the leaves of the watercress and set aside. Add the stalks – and the stock cubes if using water – to the saucepan and simmer until the potatoes are really tender, about 20 minutes.

Tip the contents of the saucepan into a liquidizer or food processor and blend until smooth, then return to the pan. Chop the watercress leaves finely and add to the soup. Season to taste with nutmeg and pepper: you may not need salt if the stock cubes are salty. Add the cream or milk, heat through and serve hot.

Serve this country soup from Normandy as a warming lunch with French bread and a board of ripe French cheeses. Or, for a winter dinner, serve it as a starter before couscous with spicy leeks and tomatoes (page 22), followed by a dark chocolate mousse.

Mushroom and pesto tartlets

SERVES 4

500 g/1 lb 2 oz puff pastry
1 egg yolk, beaten
6–8 teaspoons pesto (page 34)
8 brown mushrooms,
   thinly sliced
4 tablespoons virgin olive oil
2 tablespoons chopped fresh
   mixed herbs, or 1 tablespoon
   dried mixed herbs
salt and pepper

Preheat the oven to 220°C/425°F/Gas Mark 7. Grease four 15 cm/6 inch diameter flan tins with removable bases.

On a lightly floured surface, roll out the pastry to about 5 mm/¼ inch thick and cut into rounds about 1 cm/½ inch larger than the tins. Line the flan tins with the pastry, trim the edges and brush with beaten egg yolk. Spread a thin layer of pesto over the bottom of each pastry base.

Arrange the sliced mushrooms over the pastry, overlapping them and slanting them up around the edges. Brush liberally with olive oil, then sprinkle with the herbs and grind on some black pepper. Bake for 20–25 minutes, until the pastry is well risen and cooked through. Carefully remove the tartlets from the tins and eat as soon as possible, while they are fresh and crisp.

Serve as a first course for a supper party, followed by polenta with sun-dried tomatoes (page 18) and a green salad, and finish with a classic lemon meringue pie. Or, for lunch, serve with the mixed leaf salad with Parmesan (page 14), along with warm homemade bread.

MIXED SALAD LEAVES
with sesame dressing and shaved Parmesan

SERVES 2

2 tablespoons light soy sauce
1 tablespoon sesame oil
1 tablespoon raspberry vinegar
150 g/5 oz mixed salad leaves
(lollo rosso, lambs' lettuce,
watercress, curly endive,
radicchio, butterhead lettuce,
rocket, baby spinach)
25 g/1 oz Parmesan cheese

Whisk together the soy sauce, sesame oil and raspberry vinegar.

Put the leaves into a salad bowl and toss in the dressing. Shave the cheese over the top with the long blade of the grater, and serve at once.

This elegant salad from California goes well with most of the main dishes in this little book – especially the polenta (page 18). Or serve on its own as a light lunch with warm granary bread and a selection of cheeses.

TINY SPINACH SOUFFLÉS

MAKES 8 SMALL SOUFFLÉS

25 g/1 oz butter or margarine,
    melted
2 tablespoons finely grated
    Parmesan cheese
500 g/1 lb 2 oz fresh spinach
béchamel sauce (page 34) made
    with 25 g/1 oz butter,
    2 tablespoons flour,
    150 ml/5 fl oz milk
2 eggs, separated, plus 2 egg
    whites
5 tablespoons grated Gruyère
    cheese
freshly grated nutmeg
salt and pepper

Preheat the oven to 180°C/350°F/Gas Mark 4. Brush the melted butter evenly inside 8 small soufflé dishes (9 cm/3½ inches diameter). Taking each dish in turn, sprinkle in some of the grated Parmesan, then roll the dish around until the inside is evenly coated. This will prevent the soufflé from sticking to the sides, and give it a delicate cheesy crust.

Wash the spinach thoroughly and cook it in just the water clinging to the leaves, until tender. Drain thoroughly by pressing it into a sieve. Chop it finely and add to the béchamel sauce. Remove from the heat, add the two egg yolks, stir in the Gruyère and season with nutmeg, salt and pepper.

Put the four egg whites into a bowl and whisk until stiff. Gently fold into the sauce. Divide the mixture between the prepared soufflé dishes. Stand them in a tray of hot water and bake for 20–23 minutes, until well risen but still creamy in the centre. Serve at once.

Serve these classic French soufflés with garlic bread as a light supper for three or four people. Or serve them as a starter before penne with red and yellow pepper sauce (page 24), plus a stir-fry or a green salad. A lime sorbet would provide the perfect finale.

POLENTA WITH SUN-DRIED TOMATOES AND MOZZARELLA

SERVES 4

600 ml/1 pint vegetable stock
(page 35)
good pinch of dried herbs
125 g/4 oz part-cooked polenta
(page 36)
1–2 teaspoons cayenne pepper
salt and pepper
25 g/1 oz butter or margarine
2 tablespoons crushed sun-dried
tomatoes
½ red onion, very thinly sliced
125 g/4 oz mozzarella cheese,
thinly sliced

Bring the stock to the boil with the herbs, then trickle in the polenta, stirring all the time. Turn the heat down and simmer gently for several minutes, until the polenta is cooked through. Season to taste with cayenne, salt and pepper, and then stir in the butter or margarine. Pour into a rectangular, buttered heatproof dish and smooth the top. Leave to cool.

To serve, heat the grill. Spread the crushed sun-dried tomatoes over the cooled polenta, and cut it into 4 squares. Top each square with finely sliced red onion and cover with mozzarella. Place under the grill for 2–3 minutes, until the cheese melts. Serve immediately.

Serve this Italian dish for supper with some new potatoes and a mixed leaf salad, followed by tiramisu. I also serve it cut into tiny squares, as a nibble to go with drinks before a meal.

CHINESE NOODLES WITH BROCCOLI, GINGER AND BLACK BEAN SAUCE

SERVES 4

4 cm/1½ inches fresh ginger,
  finely grated
1 large garlic clove, crushed
2 tablespoons black bean sauce
2 tablespoons light soy sauce
4–5 tablespoons sesame oil
500 g/1 lb 2 oz broccoli
250 g/9 oz rice vermicelli or
  thin egg noodles

First make the sauce: in a small bowl, combine the ginger, garlic, black bean sauce, soy sauce and sesame oil and mix well.

Steam the broccoli until tender, about 6–7 minutes. Chop it into small pieces. Meanwhile cook the noodles in boiling water for 1–2 minutes, remove from the heat and leave to stand for a further 2 minutes, then drain thoroughly. Mix in the broccoli, then toss in the sauce. Serve at once.

To make a complete Chinese meal, serve little spring rolls to start with, and finish with an exotic fruit salad of fresh mango and lychees.

COUSCOUS WITH SPICY LEEKS AND TOMATOES

SERVES 4–6

675 g/1½ lb leeks, trimmed
2 tablespoons olive oil
3 teaspoons fresh lemon juice
600 g/1¼ lb canned chopped
    tomatoes, with juice
1 garlic clove, finely chopped
2 teaspoons each of paprika
    and cumin
a little salt
175 g/6 oz couscous (page 36)
1–2 teaspoons olive oil
1 tablespoon chopped fresh
    parsley

Cut the leeks into 2 cm/¾ inch lengths. Heat the oil in a saucepan, add the leeks and toss to coat in the oil, then add the lemon juice. Cover with a lid and cook over a low heat until the leeks 'wilt', about 15–20 minutes, stirring occasionally.

Add the tomatoes, garlic, paprika and cumin and simmer together for a further 5–6 minutes, then season to taste with a little salt.

Bring some water to the boil in a saucepan, pour in the couscous and bring back to the boil, stirring constantly. Remove from the heat, cover with a lid, and leave to steam for 5–6 minutes or until tender. Drain, then add a little olive oil and fluff up with a fork to prevent the grains from sticking together.

Pile the couscous on to a serving dish and spoon the leeks around the edge. Sprinkle with parsley and serve at once.

Couscous, a traditional Moroccan dish, makes a colourful meal preceded by watercress soup (page 10). For a Sunday lunch with friends, I also served mushroom and pesto tartlets (page 12), and we ended the meal with oranges in syrup, sprinkled with cinnamon.

PENNE WITH RED AND YELLOW PEPPER SAUCE

SERVES 4

2 large red peppers, quartered,
  stalks removed, seeded
2 large yellow peppers,
  quartered, stalks removed,
  seeded
200 ml/7 fl oz crème fraîche
500 g/1 lb 2 oz penne pasta
1 tablespoon finely chopped
  fresh coriander
grated Parmesan to serve

First, skin the peppers. You can either place them under a hot grill, skin-side up, until the skin blisters, or microwave on full power for 4–5 minutes. Leave until cool enough to handle, then peel off and discard the skins.

Purée the pepper flesh in a liquidizer or food processor and mix into the crème fraîche. This sauce needs no seasoning.

Cook the pasta (page 37), drain thoroughly and toss in the sauce. Serve in a warmed dish, with coriander sprinkled on top. Hand round the grated Parmesan in a small bowl.

This pasta dish from Sicily is at its best with warm ciabatta bread and a tossed green salad, followed by a fresh peach tart, or coffee ice cream.

CHIMICHANGAS WITH SALSA

SERVES 3–4

8 wheat tortillas, 15 cm/
   6 inches diameter
125 g/4 oz hummus
50 g/2 oz Cheddar cheese,
   grated
3 tablespoons chilli sauce
olive oil for frying

Salsa

4 canned tomatoes
¼ red onion, roughly chopped
1 fresh chilli, sliced
small bunch of parsley, chopped

First make the salsa: put all the ingredients into a liquidizer or food processor and blend briefly.

If the tortillas are a little hard, you will need to soften them so that they will not break when you wrap them around the filling. You can do this by wrapping them in a clean tea towel and then placing them in a colander over a saucepan of boiling water for 20–30 seconds. Alternatively, soften them in the microwave for a few seconds.

Put 1 tablespoon of the hummus in the centre of each tortilla, and top with grated cheese and 1 teaspoon of the chilli sauce. Wrap up into a neat parcel, secure with a toothpick or cocktail stick and fry in hot oil until golden all over. Eat at once, accompanied by the salsa.

In Mexico, chimichangas are traditionally served with salsa, a bowl of soured cream and a simple salad of crisp lettuce, tomatoes and avocado. You could follow them with bananas flambéed in rum, served with chocolate ice cream.

Butternut squash gratin

SERVES 4

Preheat the oven to 160°C/325°F/Gas Mark 3.

1 butternut squash, about
   1 kg/2¼ lb
450 ml/¾ pint béchamel sauce
   (page 34)
1–2 teaspoons chilli powder
salt and pepper
50 g/2 oz Cheddar cheese,
   grated

Peel the squash and cut into quarters, then scoop out the seeds and cut the flesh into very thin slices. Put them into a large bowl and mix with the béchamel sauce. Season with chilli powder, plenty of freshly ground black pepper, and a little salt if necessary. Put into an ovenproof dish and sprinkle with the cheese. Bake for 45 minutes and serve hot.

This dish, which I first ate in New York City, is wonderful with warm crusty bread, a mixed salad and a glass of Chardonnay. If it's cold outside, serve with a bowl of steaming rice to mop up the juices.

STIR-FRIED MANGETOUT AND MUSHROOMS

SERVES 2

1 tablespoon olive oil
3 spring onions, sliced
175 g/6 oz mangetout
1 large garlic clove, sliced
1 teaspoon grated fresh ginger
125 g/4 oz mushrooms, sliced
1–2 teaspoons chilli sauce
1 scant tablespoon light
    soy sauce
1 tablespoon sesame oil

Heat a wok or saucepan, add the oil, then add the spring onions and stir-fry briskly for 1 minute. Add the mangetout and cook for a further 2 minutes, then add the garlic and ginger. Add the mushrooms and stir-fry for about 1 minute, then add the chilli sauce, soy sauce and sesame oil. Stir well, remove from the heat and cover with a lid. Leave to steam lightly for 3–4 minutes, then serve at once while the mangetout is still crisp and bright green.

This stir-fry is perfect for a light meal, served with boiled noodles or fried rice, and followed by ripe mango slices garnished with fresh mint.

White chocolate angel gateau

SERVES 10

85 g/3 oz self-raising flour
2 teaspoons cream of tartar
175 g/6 oz caster sugar
6 egg whites
¼ teaspoon salt
1 tablespoon lemon juice
1 teaspoon vanilla essence

Filling
275 g/10 oz white chocolate, chopped
275 g/10 oz light cream cheese
3 egg whites
85 g/3 oz caster sugar

Preheat the oven to 190°C/375°F/Gas Mark 5. Grease and flour a 20 cm/8 inch round cake tin. Sift the flour, add half of the cream of tartar and sift again; set aside. Sift the sugar and set aside.

Whisk the egg whites until they form soft peaks, then add the salt and the rest of the cream of tartar. Beat in the sugar, 2 tablespoons at a time, then add the lemon juice and vanilla. Fold in the flour lightly, 2 tablespoons at a time. Turn into the prepared cake tin and bake for 20 minutes. Turn the heat down to 160°C/325°F/Gas Mark 3 and cook for a further 20 minutes. Leave in the tin on a wire rack for 10 minutes, then carefully turn out and leave to cool completely.

For the filling, melt the white chocolate in a bowl set over a pan of simmering water. Mash the cream cheese and stir into the melted chocolate. Whisk the egg whites until they form stiff peaks, then gradually whisk in the sugar until very stiff and shiny. Fold into the cream cheese and white chocolate mixture.

Slice the cake into four layers and spread each layer with some of the filling. Stack up the gateau, and dust the top with icing sugar.

For a vegetarian dinner party, start with mushroom and pesto tartlets (page 12), and follow with penne with red and yellow pepper sauce (page 24) served with stir-fried mangetout and mushrooms (page 30). Then linger over the mixed leaf salad, and finish with this exquisite angel gateau that my American mother used to make.

The Basics

Béchamel Sauce

MAKES 450 ml/¾ PINT

40 g/1½ oz butter or margarine
40 g/1½ oz plain flour
450 ml/¾ pint milk
freshly grated nutmeg
salt and pepper

Put the butter, flour and milk into a heavy-bottomed saucepan and beat continuously with a wire whisk over a medium heat until the sauce thickens. Bring to the boil, now stirring with a wooden spoon, and simmer gently for 5–6 minutes to allow the flour to cook. Season to taste with nutmeg, salt and pepper.

Pesto

1 large bunch of fresh basil
2 large garlic cloves, crushed
85 g/3 oz pine nuts
50 g/2 oz Parmesan cheese,
    finely grated
150 ml/5 fl oz olive oil

Put all the ingredients into a liquidizer or food processor and blend until smooth. Store in small airtight jars in the refrigerator for up to 1 week. Pesto also freezes well.

VEGETABLE STOCK

Making your own vegetable stock is an excellent way of using up vegetable trimmings, and makes a tasty stock for soups. However, vegetable stock cubes are a perfectly acceptable alternative.

Scraps of carrot, onion, leek, cabbage, tomato, Jerusalem artichoke, broccoli, cauliflower – and even potato peelings – can all go into the pot. Add any other spare vegetables, cover with cold water, then add a little sea salt, some black peppercorns, 1–2 bay leaves and a good pinch of mixed dried herbs. Bring to the boil, then lower the heat and simmer gently, covered, for 45 minutes. Remove from the heat and leave to stand until cold.

Strain the stock, taste, and if you like, boil for a further 10 minutes or so to concentrate the flavour. Stock can be kept for up to 3 days in the refrigerator.

POLENTA

Polenta is a yellow, grainy meal made from maize; it is a popular staple north of the River Po in Italy, from Piedmont to the Veneto. It provides a simple, wholesome base to which you can add favourite flavours. Traditional polenta takes 40–50 minutes to cook and needs constant stirring, but part-cooked 'instant' polenta is widely available.

COUSCOUS

Couscous is of Berber origin and is made of tiny pellets of semolina coated with fine wheat flour. In North African cooking, couscous is steamed over the vegetables (or meat) as they cook, but you can now buy part-cooked couscous which is incredibly quick and easy to make.

COOKING PASTA

Bring a large saucepan of water to the boil. Add the pasta, bring back to the boil and stir. Remove from the heat, cover with a lid and leave to stand for 8–10 minutes, until the pasta is 'al dente'. Test by biting a small piece of pasta – it should be tender, but should remain slightly firm in the centre. Add a little salt and stir. This method not only stops the water boiling all over the stove, it also prevents the pasta from hardening as it cooks.

GINGER

Keep peeled fresh ginger in a plastic bag in the freezer, and grate from frozen every time you need it.

Classic Cooking

STARTERS

Lesley Waters A former chef and now a popular television cook, appearing regularly on *Ready Steady Cook* and *Can't Cook Won't Cook*. Author of several cookery books.

VEGETABLE SOUPS

Elisabeth Luard Cookery writer for the *Sunday Telegraph Magazine* and author of *European Peasant Food* and *European Festival Food*, which won a Glenfiddich Award.

GOURMET SALADS

Sonia Stevenson The first woman chef in the UK to be awarded a Michelin star, at the Horn of Plenty in Devon. Author of *The Magic of Saucery* and *Fresh Ways with Fish*.

FISH AND SHELLFISH

Gordon Ramsay Chef/proprietor of London's Aubergine restaurant, recently awarded its second Michelin star, and author of *A Passion for Flavour*.

CHICKEN, DUCK AND GAME

Nick Nairn Chef/patron of Braeval restaurant near Aberfoyle in Scotland, whose BBC-TV series *Wild Harvest* was last summer's most successful cookery series, accompanied by a book.

LIVERS, SWEETBREADS AND KIDNEYS

Simon Hopkinson Former chef/patron at London's Bibendum restaurant, columnist and author of *Roast Chicken and Other Stories* and *The Prawn Cocktail Years*.

VEGETARIAN

Rosamond Richardson Author of several vegetarian titles, including *The Great Green Cookbook* and *Food from Green Places*.

PASTA

Joy Davies One of the creators of *BBC Good Food Magazine*, she has been food editor of *She, Woman* and *Options* and written for the *Guardian, Daily Telegraph* and *Harpers & Queen*.

CHEESE DISHES

Rose Elliot The UK's most successful vegetarian cookery writer and author of many books, including *Not Just a Load of Old Lentils* and *The Classic Vegetarian Cookbook*.

POTATO DISHES

Patrick McDonald Former chef/patron of the acclaimed Epicurean restaurant in Cheltenham, and food consultant to Sir Rocco Forte Hotels.

BISTRO

Anne Willan Founder and director of La Varenne Cookery School in Burgundy and West Virginia. Author of many books and a specialist in French cuisine.

ITALIAN

Anna Del Conte Author of several books on Italian food, including *The Gastronomy of Italy, Secrets from an Italian Kitchen* and *The Classic Food of Northern Italy* (chosen as the 1996 Guild of Food Writers Book of the Year).

VIETNAMESE
Nicole Routhier One of the United States' most popular cookery writers, her books include *Cooking Under Wraps, Nicole Routhier's Fruit Cookbook* and the award-winning *The Foods of Vietnam*.

MALAYSIAN
Jill Dupleix One of Australia's best known cookery writers and broadcasters, with columns in the *Sydney Morning Herald* and *Elle*. Her books include *New Food* and *Allegro al dente*.

PEKING CUISINE
Helen Chen Author of *Chinese Home Cooking,* she learned to cook traditional Peking dishes from her mother, Joyce Chen, the *grande dame* of Chinese cooking in the United States.

STIR-FRIES
Kay Fairfax A writer and broadcaster whose books include *100 Great Stir-fries, Homemade* and *The Australian Christmas Book*.

NOODLES
Terry Durack Australia's most widely read restaurant critic and co-editor of the *Sydney Morning Herald Good Food Guide*. He is the author of *YUM*, a book of stories and recipes.

NORTH INDIAN CURRIES
Pat Chapman Founded the Curry Club in 1982. A regular broadcaster on television and radio, he is the author of 20 books, which have sold more than 1 million copies.

GRILLS AND BARBECUES
Brian Turner Chef/patron of Turner's in Knightsbridge and one of Britain's most popular food broadcasters; he appears frequently on *Ready Steady Cook, Food and Drink* and many other television programmes.

SUMMER AND WINTER CASSEROLES
Anton Edelmann Maître Chef des Cuisines at the Savoy Hotel, London. Author of six cookery books, he has also appeared on television.

TRADITIONAL PUDDINGS
Tessa Bramley Chef/patron of the acclaimed Old Vicarage restaurant in Ridgeway, Derbyshire and author of *The Instinctive Cook*.

DECORATED CAKES
Jane Asher Author of several cookery books and a novel. She has also appeared in her own television series, *Jane Asher's Christmas* (1995).

FAVOURITE CAKES
Mary Berry One of Britain's leading cookery writers, her numerous books include *Mary Berry's Ultimate Cake Book*. She has made many television and radio appearances.

ICE CREAMS AND SEMI FREDDI
Ann and Franco Taruschio Owners of the renowned Walnut Tree Inn near Abergavenny in Wales, soon to appear in a television series, *Franco and Friends: Food from the Walnut Tree*. They have written three books together.

Text © Rosamond Richardson 1997

Rosamond Richardson has asserted her right to be
identified as the author of this Work.

Photographs © Philip Wilkins 1997

First published in 1997 by
George Weidenfeld & Nicolson
The Orion Publishing Group
Orion House
5 Upper St Martin's Lane
London WC2H 9EA

British Library Cataloguing-in-Publication data
A catalogue record for this book is available from
the British Library

ISBN 0 297 82334 5

Designed by Lucy Holmes
Edited by Maggie Ramsay
Food styling by Louise Pickford
Typesetting by Tiger Typeset